WHAT DO YOU FIND AT THE LIBRARY?

by Mirabella Mendez
illustrated by Nancy Doniger

 Harcourt

Orlando   Boston   Dallas   Chicago   San Diego

Visit *The Learning Site!*

www.harcourtschool.com

You find lots of
books.

You find magazines.

You find a story
circle.

You find a quiet corner.

You find a computer.

You find people who help.

Then you find your
favorite book!